Pebble® Plus

Creepy Crawlers

Crickets

by Nikki Bruno Clapper

Gail Saunders-Smith, PhD, Consulting Editor
Consultant: Orin A. McMonigle
Editor in Chief
Invertebrates Magazine

CAPSTONE PRESS
a capstone imprint

Pebble Plus is published by Capstone Press,
1710 Roe Crest Drive, North Mankato, Minnesota 56003.
www.capstonepub.com

Library of Congress Cataloging-in-Publication Data
Clapper, Nikki Bruno, author.
Crickets/by Nikki Bruno Clapper.
pages cm.—(Pebble Plus. Creepy Crawlers)
Summary: "Simple text and full-color photographs introduce crickets"—Provided by publisher.
Audience: Ages 4–8
Audience: K to grade 3
ISBN 978-1-4914-6217-1 (library binding)
ISBN 978-1-4914-6229-4 (ebook pdf)
1. Crickets—Juvenile literature. I. Title. II. Series: Pebble Plus. Creepy Crawlers.
QL508.G8C53 2016
595.7'26—dc23   2015008492

Editorial Credits
Michelle Bisson and Jeni Wittrock, editors; Juliette Peters, designer; Katy LaVigne, production specialist

Photo Credits
Getty Images: Science Source/Coleman Ray, 13; James P. Rowan, 5; Minden Pictures: NPL/Premaphotos, 19; Newscom: imago stock & people, 15, Minden Pictures/Vincent Grafhorst, 17; Orin McMonigle, 9; Shutterstock: alexsvirid, 11, Anatolich, 7, D. Kucharski K. Kucharska, 21 (inset), Melinda Fawver, 1, netsuthep, 21, pattara puttiwong, cover

Design Element
Shutterstock: vlastas66

Note to Parents and Teachers

The Creepy Crawlers set supports national science standards related to biology and life science. This book describes and illustrates crickets. The images support early readers in understanding the text. The repetition of words and phrases helps early readers learn new words. This book also introduces early readers to subject-specific vocabulary words, which are defined in the Glossary section. Early readers may need assistance to read some words and to use the Table of Contents, Glossary, Read More, Internet Sites, Critical Thinking Using the Common Core, and Index sections of the book.

Printed in the United States of America in North Mankato, Minnesota.
042015   008823CGF15

Table of Contents

Noise in the Night

Loud chirping sounds
fill the summer night.
Thousands of crickets
are calling for mates.

Crickets are insects. They are related to grasshoppers and katydids. These insects have long back legs. They jump away from predators.

Crickets have strong back legs.

Fields, Meadows, and More

Crickets live all around the world. They are common in fields and forests. You can also find them in deserts and caves.

cave crickets

A Cricket's Body

A cricket has a round head.

Its antennae are as long as

its body—or even longer.

Some crickets have wings.

Others have no wings.

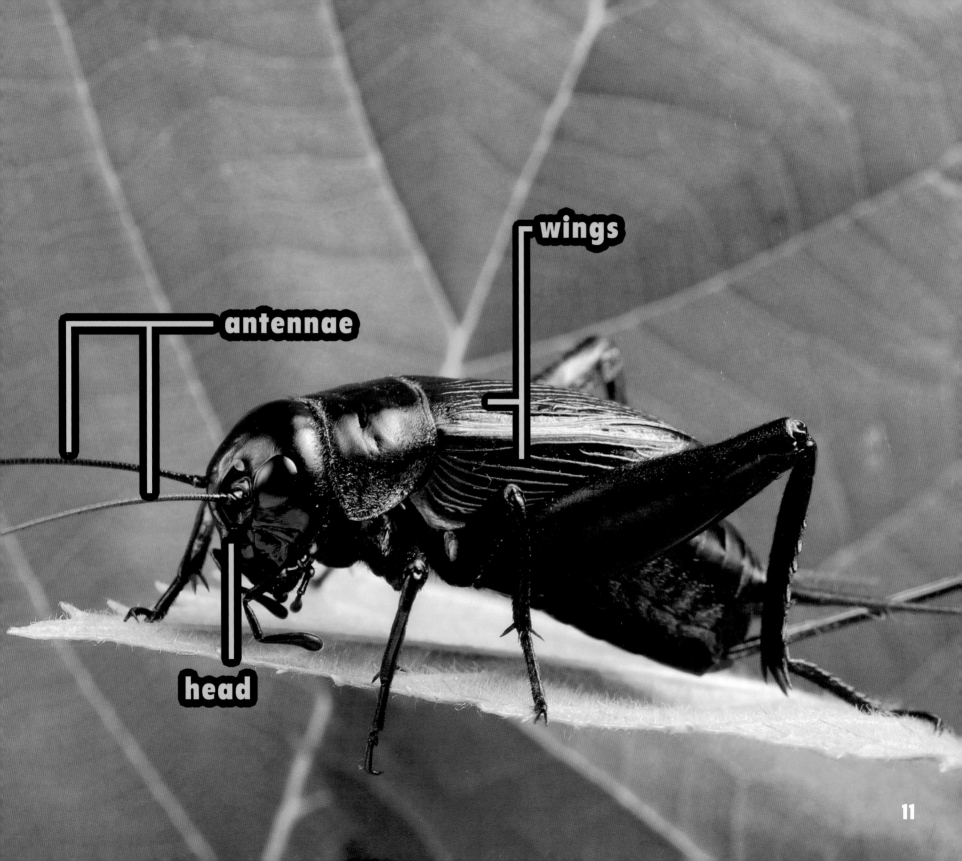

wings

antennae

head

Female crickets have a body part called an ovipositor.

It looks like a tail.

Females use it to lay eggs.

oviposit

A cricket has five eyes. The two largest eyes are compound eyes. They see in many directions. A cricket's ears are on its legs.

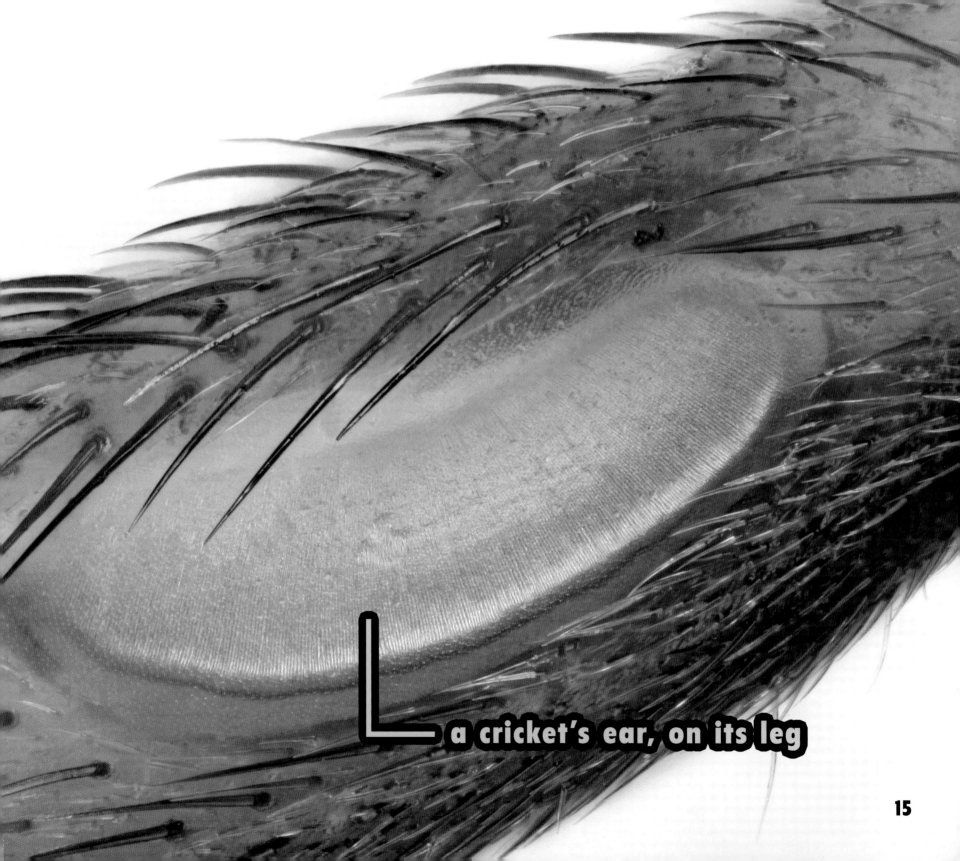

La cricket's ear, on its leg

Eating and Chirping

Crickets eat plants, fungi, and other insects. Most crickets are nocturnal. During the day they hide from predators.

a cricket eating another cricket

Only adult male crickets chirp. They rub their wings together to make noise. When the temperature rises, crickets chirp faster.

front wings

A Cricket's Life

Female crickets lay hundreds of eggs. Baby crickets hatch from the eggs. Crickets shed their skin as they grow. They live for about six months.

cricket egg

Glossary

antenna—a feeler on an insect's head; more than one antenna are antennae

compound eyes—compound eyes are made up of lots of lenses; they are good for seeing fast-moving things

desert—a dry area with little rain

fungus—a type of organism that is like a plant but has no leaves, flowers, or roots; a group of fungus is fungi

insect—a small animal with a hard outer shell, six legs, three body sections, and two antennae; most insects have wings

katydid—a large, green insect that is like a grasshopper

mate—one partner of a pair of animals

nocturnal—active at night and resting during the day

ovipositor—a long, pointed body part on a female cricket through which eggs pass

predator—an animal that hunts other animals for food

shed—to drop or fall off; insects shed their skin as they grow

Read More

Bodden, Valerie. *Crickets.* Creepy Creatures. Mankato, Minn.: Creative Education, 2011.

Martin, Isabel. *Insects: A Question and Answer Book.* Animal Kingdom Questions and Answers. North Mankato, Minn.: Capstone Press, 2015.

Silverman, Buffy. *Can You Tell a Cricket from a Grasshopper?* Animal Look-Alikes. Minneapolis: Lerner, 2012.

Internet Sites

FactHound offers a safe, fun way to find Internet sites related to this book. All of the sites on FactHound have been researched by our staff.

Here's all you do:

Visit *www.facthound.com*

Type in this code: 9781491462171

Check out projects, games and lots more at
www.capstonekids.com

Critical Thinking
Using the Common Core

1. Why do adult male crickets chirp? (Key Ideas and Details)

2. Only female crickets have an ovipositor. What does this body part do? (Key Ideas and Details)

Index

Word Count: 191
Grade: 1
Early-Intervention Level: 18